D1605270

The Countries

Romania

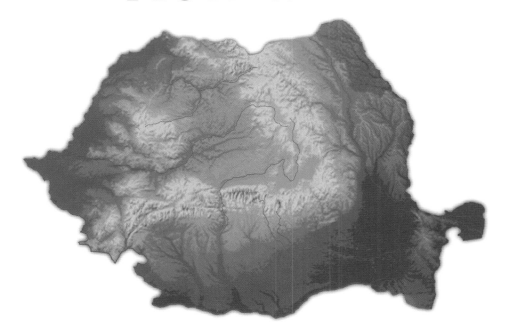

Kristin Van Cleaf

ABDO Publishing Company

visit us at
www.abdopublishing.com

Published by ABDO Publishing Company, 8000 West 78th Street, Edina, Minnesota 55439.
Copyright © 2008 by Abdo Consulting Group, Inc. International copyrights reserved in all
countries. No part of this book may be reproduced in any form without written permission from the
publisher. The Checkerboard Library™ is a trademark and logo of ABDO Publishing Company.

Printed in the United States.

Interior Photos: Alamy pp. 5, 6, 9, 10, 14, 25, 26, 27; AP Images pp. 28, 37; Corbis pp. 11, 13,
    18, 19, 21, 22, 33, 35, 36; Getty Images p. 29; Peter Arnold p. 31

Editors: Rochelle Baltzer, Heidi M.D. Elston
Art Direction & Maps: Neil Klinepier

Library of Congress Cataloging-in-Publication Data

Van Cleaf, Kristin, 1976-
  Romania / Kristin Van Cleaf.
      p. cm. -- (The countries)
  Includes index.
  ISBN 978-1-59928-785-0
  1. Romania--Juvenile literature. I. Title.

  DR217.V36 2007
  949.8--dc22

                            2007010182

Contents

Bună Ziua!

Hello from Romania! Nestled in eastern Europe, Romania is covered with curving mountains and rolling hills. The famous Danube River snakes along its southern border. And, the Black Sea lies to the east of the country.

Romania has much to offer, including fascinating **architecture**. Historic sites have been preserved throughout the country. People visit Romania's ancient castles and fortresses that once served as defenses against invaders. Bran Castle, often called Dracula's Castle, was made popular by Bram Stoker's book titled *Dracula*.

Modern architecture, such as the Palace of **Parliament** in Bucharest (BOO-kuh-rehst), is also found throughout Romania. The **communist** government had the Palace of Parliament built in the 1980s. Yet today, it stands as a symbol of **democracy** and the country's advancements.

Romania was ruled by other nations for many years. And, an underdeveloped **economy** kept many of the people poor.

But since the 1990s, Romania has been a united, independent **republic**. And, the **economy** is slowly growing.

Despite invasions and economic troubles, Romanians have maintained a strong **culture**. The people continue to celebrate their **heritage**. Folk arts and crafts still shine.

Bună ziua from Romania!

Fast Facts

OFFICIAL NAME: Romania
CAPITAL: Bucharest

LAND
- Area: 91,700 square miles (237,500 sq km)
- Mountain Ranges: Carpathian Mountains, Transylvanian Alps
- Highest Point: Moldoveanu 8,346 feet (2,544 m)
- Major Rivers: Danube, Prut, Mureş, Olt, Siret, Ialomiţa, Someş

PEOPLE
- Population: 22,276,056 (July 2007 estimate)
- Major Cities: Bucharest, Constanţa, Iaşi
- Official Language: Romanian
- Religions: Eastern Orthodoxy, Protestantism, Roman Catholicism

GOVERNMENT
- Form: Republic
- Head of State: President
- Head of Government: Prime minister
- Legislature: Bicameral parliament
- Nationhood: December 30, 1947

ECONOMY
- Agricultural Products: Wheat, corn, barley, sugar beets, sunflower seeds, potatoes, grapes, eggs, sheep
- Mining Products: Bauxite, coal, copper, gold, iron ore, lead, silver, zinc
- Manufactured Products: Textiles, footwear, light machinery, construction materials, chemicals
- Money: Leu (1 leu = 100 bani)

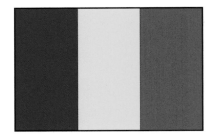

Romania's flag

Romanian lei

Timeline

800 BC	Dacians first settle in Romania's Transylvania region
AD 107	Romans conquer the Dacians
1300s	The independent regions of Moldavia and Walachia are formed
1861	Moldavia and Walachia unite
1878	Major European powers recognize Romania's independence
1881	Romania becomes a kingdom
1916	Romania joins the Allies in World War I
1944	Romania joins the Allies in World War II
1947	The Soviet Union gains control of Romania
1965	Romania declares itself independent of the Soviet Union
1989	An anticommunist revolution forces out the communist-led government
1990	Free elections are held in Romania
1991	Romania's constitution is adopted
2004	Romania joins NATO
2007	Romania joins the European Union

Land of the Romans

Around 800 BC, people called Dacians settled in Romania's Transylvania region. There, they farmed and traded. They also developed their metalworking skills.

In AD 107, the Romans conquered Dacia. Roman **culture** and Latin Christianity spread throughout the area. Soon, Dacia became known as Romania. Romania suffered invasions by many tribes from 271 to the 1100s. As a result, Romania became a mix of cultures.

The people of eastern Romania formed Moldavia in the 1300s. To the south was another independent state, Walachia. Each state was ruled by a prince. So, they were called principalities.

These independent states did not last long. The **Ottoman Empire** conquered Walachia in 1476 and Moldavia in 1504. Life became more difficult for the peasants, who were already very poor. The empire sent Greeks known as Phanariots to govern the principalities. The Phanariots treated the peasants harshly and charged large taxes.

In 1821, the **Ottoman Empire** replaced the Phanariots with native princes. Then in 1829, Russians occupied the Romanian principalities. Russian leaders established a **constitution** for Walachia and Moldavia. It granted power to an assembly of nobles in each territory. The Russians left in 1834.

Emperor Trajan led the Romans into Dacia.

In January 1859, both Moldavia and Walachia elected Alexandru Ion Cuza as prince. The two areas united in 1861 and later adopted the name *Romania*.

Prince Alexandru made many reforms. He seized land from nobles and monasteries and gave it to peasants. And, he increased the number of free schools for the poor. However, wealthy Romanians disliked Prince Alexandru's actions. They forced him to resign in 1866.

King Carol I served as Romania's first king from 1881 to 1914.

Karl of Hohenzollern-Sigmaringen replaced Prince Alexandru. He took the name Prince Carol. Romania declared its independence in May 1877. In 1878, the major European nations recognized this. Romania became a kingdom in 1881, so Prince Carol became King Carol I.

Romania's **economy** improved. But, only the wealthy benefited. The peasants revolted in 1888 and 1907. But, the Romanian Army defeated these uprisings. In 1914, King Carol died and was replaced by King Ferdinand.

King Ferdinand kept Romania out of **World War I** until 1916. At that time, Romania joined the **Allies**. The Allies won, and Romania received the lands of Banat, Bukovina, and Transylvania. The country doubled in size!

In 1927, King Ferdinand died. His son took the throne as King Carol II three years later. The country worried as it became clear that **World War II** was coming. So, King Carol II made an **alliance** with Germany. In exchange for protection, Romania lost large portions of land. The people protested. So in September 1940, King Carol II gave up the throne.

Allied flags of World War I

King Carol II's young son Michael became king next. However, General Ion Antonescu ruled. As a result, Romania joined the war on Germany's side. But in 1944, King Michael overthrew Antonescu, and Romania joined the **Allies**. Under Soviet protection, Romanian **communists** forced King Michael to resign in 1947.

With communists in control, Romania was a **Soviet satellite**. But, Romanians did not like the Soviet influence on their government, educational system, and **economy**.

In 1965, Romania declared itself independent of the Soviet Union. Romanian Communist Party leader Nicolae Ceausescu (chow-SHEHS-koo) named himself president of Romania in 1974.

By 1980, Romania's economy had slowed. The people had less access to food, energy, and other necessities. And, working conditions were poor. Romanians became very unhappy with their president. On December 16, 1989, fighting broke out between the people and government forces. The police responded violently, and more than 1,000 people died.

Ceausescu was captured and executed on December 25. A group called the National Salvation Front (NSF) took control of the government. The NSF lessened limitations on Romanians and gave them more access to food and energy.

Free elections were held in 1990. The people elected Ion Iliescu as president. And, the NSF won a large majority. However following protests, the NSF government stepped down in late 1991. New elections held the next year again placed Iliescu in the presidency.

In 1996, Emil Constantinescu became president. Iliescu was elected president again in 2000. Four years later, Romania joined **NATO**. Also in 2004, Romanians elected Traian Basescu as president. On January 1, 2007, Romania joined the **European Union**.

Romanians experienced mixed emotions about the fall of Ceausescu and communism. Some grieved, while others were overjoyed that their country was free.

Land and Climate

Romania is surrounded by several countries and one body of water. Ukraine borders Romania to the north and the east. Romania shares its northeastern border with Moldova. The Black Sea is to the east. Bulgaria is Romania's southern neighbor. And Serbia is southwest, while Hungary lies west.

Romanians take advantage of all that the country's mountains have to offer.

Romania is a country of varied beauty. It is made up of mountains, hills, and plains. The central part of the country is known as the Transylvanian **Basin**. This hilly area is cut by the Mureş (MOO-rehsh) and Someş (soh-MEHSH) river valleys.

The Carpathian Mountains curve around the Transylvanian Basin. These mountains swing down from north to south. They become the Transylvanian Alps toward the center of the country, in a line from east to west. Moldoveanu is Romania's highest peak. It stands 8,346 feet (2,544 m) high.

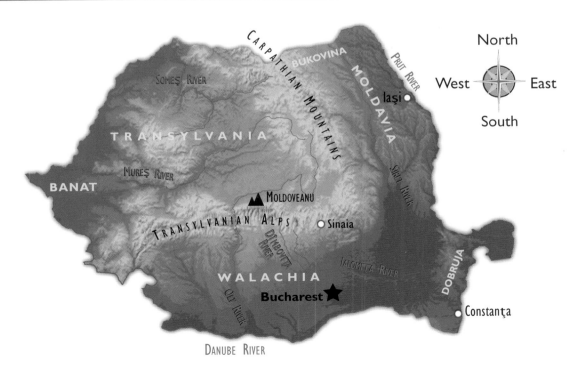

The country's largest region, Transylvania, covers central and northwestern Romania. This area includes the Transylvanian **Basin** and much of the country's mountains.

East of the Carpathians lies Moldavia. This region is made up of foothills and grassy plains. Walachia is similar and lies to the south. Bukovina is a heavily forested area northeast of Transylvania. The Dobruja (DAW-broo-jah) region is along the Black Sea. And, Banat and its plains are located southwest of Transylvania.

The country's main river is the Danube. It flows from west to east, into the Black Sea. Most of the rivers in Romania flow into the Danube. These include the Olt, Ialomiţa, Siret, and Prut rivers. About 2,500 lakes add to Romania's beauty.

Romania's climate is varied and somewhat **humid**. The mountains are colder and wetter than the plains. Springs tend to be short, with floods along the Danube. Summers are dry and hot. July's average temperature is 73 degrees Fahrenheit (23°C). Winters are cold, cloudy, and snowy. The average January temperature is 27 degrees Fahrenheit (-3°C).

Rainfall

AVERAGE YEARLY RAINFALL

Inches		Centimeters
Under 20		Under 50
20–40		50–100
40–60		100–150
Over 60		Over 150

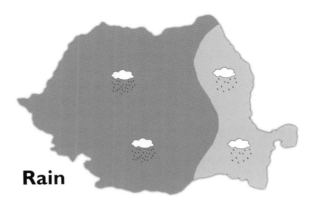

Rain

Temperature

AVERAGE TEMPERATURE

Fahrenheit		Celsius
Over 76°		Over 24°
65°–76°		18°–24°
54°–65°		12°–18°
32°–54°		0°–12°
21°–32°		-6°–0°
Below 21°		Below -6°

Winter

North
West East
South

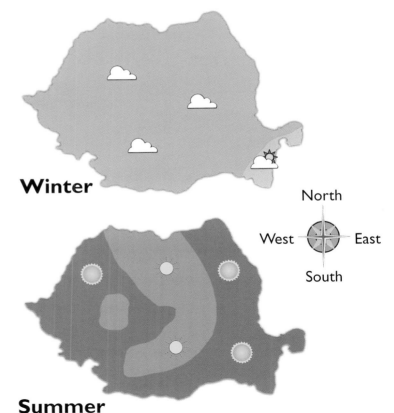

Summer

The Great Outdoors

Forests cover about one-fourth of Romania's land. Oak trees grow most commonly in the lowlands. Beeches and coniferous trees are more common in mountainous areas.

People have lived on Romanian land for hundreds of years. So, building and farming have destroyed much of the country's native plants. However, there are pastures and grassy plains toward the mountain peaks.

Many animals live among the forests. Brown bears, red deers, foxes, lynxes, wolves, martens, and wild pigs are common forest

Fishing is important to Romania's economy. Most of the fish caught in Romania come from the Danube River.

animals. One of the more rare species is the chamois (SHA-mee). This small, horned animal is similar to a goat. And, passersby often hear songbirds.

The Black Sea and Romania's rivers, such as the Danube, also contain wildlife. Birds and fish are found near or in the waters. These water sources provide good fishing. Most catches are eaten fresh. The rest are processed and canned. And, people collect sturgeon eggs for caviar. Many people consider caviar a luxury food.

The Carpathian Mountains have some of the highest populations of wolves and bears in Europe.

The Romanian government has created protective sites for animals and their surroundings. These include about a dozen natural reservations and more than 100 parks and animal preserves. There is also a wildlife preserve where the Danube meets the Black Sea. And, forested parks are found near every large city.

Romanians

Romanians are descended from peoples such as Romans, Dacians, Goths, Slavs, and Huns. Today, about 90 percent of the country's citizens are Romanian. Hungarians, Roma, Jews, Germans, Ukranians, and Turks also live there.

Most people speak Romanian, the national language. It is the only eastern European language related to Latin. Latin was the language of the Romans. Romanian also has Slavic, Turkish, Hungarian, German, and Albanian influences. Hungarian and German are also spoken throughout.

Romania has one of the lowest standards of living in Europe. Most people earn just enough money to buy food, clothing, and housing. About 25 percent of Romanians own a television. Around 15 percent can afford an automobile.

Romanian cities are a mix of both old and new. Unfortunately, many cities are experiencing a housing shortage. So, people often live in crowded apartments.

Simple, small, wooden homes are common in rural Romania. The people decorate them with colorful handmade rugs and plates. They also add wood carvings to furniture and fences.

Rural life centers on farming and traditional crafts and customs.

Today, Romanians enjoy religious freedom. Most of them belong to the Eastern **Orthodox** churches. Many Hungarians and Germans are **Protestant** or Roman Catholic.

Romanian foods have many foreign influences. A typical breakfast consists of eggs, cheese, bread, and coffee. Lunch starts with soup. After this, meat, potatoes, and a vegetable are served.

Many Romanians enjoy eating grilled meats. Some examples are cylinder-shaped meatballs called *mititei* and sausages called *patricieni*. A favorite dish is a cornmeal mush called *mamaliga*, which is served like mashed potatoes. Plum brandy called *tzuica* (tsooee-kuh) is a common drink. And, pastries are popular desserts.

Most schooling in Romania is free. And, children must attend school from ages 6 to 16. Students spend eight years in elementary school. Most learn English at this young age.

Students complete a test to determine what they will study in secondary school. They often take courses in teaching or the arts. Or, they learn **vocational** or advanced technical skills. The top elementary school graduates take courses to prepare them for college. Romania has seven universities.

Chiftelute de Varza

Romanians serve these cabbage pancakes as a main dish.

- 1 small cabbage
- 1 egg
- salt and pepper

- 3 tablespoons lard or oil
- 1 teaspoon mixed chopped parsley and dill
- 2 to 3 tablespoons flour or bread crumbs

Slice cabbage into thin, matchstick-size strips. Rub some salt into the cabbage and scald with water. Drain well and grind. Next, mix the cabbage with the egg, flour, parsley and dill, and a dash of salt and pepper. Form pancakes from the mixture. Finally, coat the pancakes with flour or bread crumbs and fry in hot lard or oil.

AN IMPORTANT NOTE TO THE CHEF: Always have an adult help with the preparation and cooking of food. Never use kitchen utensils or appliances without adult permission and supervision.

LANGUAGE

English	Romanian
Hello	Bună ziua (boo-nuh ZEE-wah)
Yes	Da (dah)
No	Nu (noo)
Please	Vă rog (vuh ROHG)
Thank you	Vă mulţumesc (vuh MUHLL-tsoo-mehsk)

Communism to Democracy

Communism in Romania ended in 1989. In 1991, government leaders created a new **constitution** that established Romania as a **republic**.

Today, citizens who are at least 18 years old may vote for government leaders. The people directly elect a president to serve a five-year term. This person is the head of state and of the military.

The president can declare **martial law** in an emergency. He or she also nominates the head of government, the prime minister. The prime minister and the cabinet ministers are responsible for putting policy into effect.

The legislative branch is a **parliament** made up of the Chamber of Deputies and the Senate. The Chamber has 332 seats, and the Senate has 137. Direct, popular votes appoint members of both houses to four-year terms.

Romania's Palace of Parliament houses the Chamber of Deputies and the Senate. This grand building can be spotted from anywhere in Bucharest.

The judicial branch is made up of courts at different levels. The Supreme Court of Justice is the highest court. The president appoints its members. There are also county, local, and military courts. Local court decisions can be appealed to county courts.

Growing Economy

Before **World War II**, Romania had an agriculture-based **economy**. Then, the **communists** concentrated on industry. Today, the government is working toward a **free enterprise** economy.

Romania has many natural resources. About 60 percent of the land is rich farmland. Another 25 percent is forested, which provides timber. And, the mountains contain rich mineral deposits.

Romanians produce construction materials, wood and petroleum products, iron, and steel. They also build farm, factory, and mining machinery. And, they process foods and make shoes and clothing.

Romania's main exports are lumber, cement, foods, clothing, and shoes. Romania imports and

Woodworking is an old tradition in Romania.

exports machinery, chemicals, and fuels. It also imports coal, iron ore, and cotton.

In Romania more sheep are raised than any other farm animal.

Agriculture still has a place in Romania's **economy**. Farmers produce large amounts of corn, wheat, barley, rye, and oats. They also grow fruits, such as grapes. Common vegetable crops are peas, beans, lentils, and potatoes. Farmers also raise sheep, poultry, cattle, horses, and pigs.

Trade and transportation employ many Romanians. Other service areas include housing, health care, education, and defense. Tourism has also become important to the economy.

Staying Connected

Automobile traffic still competes with animal-drawn carts.

In Romania, public transportation is fairly inexpensive. So, buses are a common form of transportation inside cities. Buses also help people living in villages get to the cities. Donkey-drawn carts and bicycles are still common in rural areas.

The train system provides most long-distance transportation. However, many trains are in bad shape and do not provide heat in winter.

Romania's main airport is in Bucharest. Flights deliver passengers to both domestic and international destinations.

Boats also provide international travel. The Danube River is a vital transportation route.

More than 1,000 newspapers and magazines are published in Romania. Both **satellite** and state-owned television services are available. And, radio programs are broadcast in many languages. Most Romanians own a telephone. However, some rural areas do not provide telephone service. Also, more than 4 million Romanians surf the Internet.

About 40 daily newspapers are printed in Romania.

Discover Romania

Romania's capital is Bucharest. The city lies on the Dîmboviţa River. Bucharest is Romania's **economic**, administrative, **cultural**, industrial, and governmental center. It is also home to the country's largest university. And, there are several art and science academies, as well as many research institutes.

Theater and the national orchestra have long been a part of Bucharest. The city also has many museums. Its Village Museum is of special interest. It is made up of houses and buildings from the surrounding countryside. Visitors can view village buildings that were typical in the 1600s through the 1900s.

Romania's second-largest city is Constanţa in the southeast. Located on the Black Sea, this city is the country's main seaport. This busy port serves Ukraine, Russia, and Turkey, as well as ports on the Mediterranean Sea. Constanţa is full of rich art and culture, too. Visitors can take advantage of the city's museums, theaters, and shops.

Iaşi (YAHSH) is Romania's third-largest city. It lies in the northeast on the Bahlui River. Iaşi is a growing industrial center as well as a **cultural** center. It is home to Romania's oldest university, Alexandru Ioan Cuza University, which was founded in 1860. Other historic buildings, such as the Palace of Culture, draw visitors from around the globe.

In Romanian, the city of Bucharest is called Bucuresti.

Celebrations and Traditions

Many Romanians observe Christian holidays such as Christmas and Easter. But, most celebrate Easter according to the **Orthodox** calendar.

Romanians also observe national holidays. On December 1, National Day marks the union of Romania and Transylvania. And, New Year's is one of the most popular holidays.

Romanian festivals are steeped in tradition. For Mărţişor on March 1, men give women and girls small brooches. In July, Bucharest of Old is held to celebrate the city's history. People parade in clothing from the 1800s. Traditional foods and musical performances are enjoyed by all.

On the third Sunday in July, single men and women attend the Maidens' Fair. Villagers wearing traditional clothing walk to the top of Gaina Mountain in Transylvania. There, they dance and feast while looking for a husband or a wife.

In August, Dance at Prislop celebrates the connection between Transylvania, Moldova, and Maramures. Romanians wear traditional clothing and dance and feast in Prislop Pass in the Carpathian Mountains. The Romanian Folk Art Festival is also in August. There, well-known folk artists offer lessons in traditional crafts.

In autumn, Sambra Oilor marks the return of sheep herds from the mountains. And, a wine festival celebrates the beginning of the grape harvest. Romanians love any excuse to gather with friends and family!

Festivals, holidays, and weddings are especially important to rural Romanians. They proudly dress in colorful costumes for these events.

Lasting Culture

Romania has a beautiful **culture** that has survived hundreds of years and many foreign invasions. When **communists** took over the government, they put many limitations on art and literature. Today, Romanians enjoy artistic freedom. As a result, the country's arts have flourished. Much of Romania's art is preserved in museums throughout the country.

Born in 1876, Constantin Brancuşi (BRAHN-koosh) is one of the best-known Romanian sculptors. He carved elegant shapes from wood and marble. Two of his famous pieces are *Table of Silence* and *Endless Column*.

Literature in Romania began in the 1400s as translations of religious texts. After this, Romanians started writing histories. In the 1800s, Iancu Văcărescu (vuh-kuh-REH-skoo) wrote lyric poems. He is known as the Father of Romanian Poetry.

Romania has a variety of breathtaking **architecture**, both old and modern. Peles Castle, located in Sinaia (see-NEYE-uh), was built in the late 1800s. Many people consider it Europe's most beautiful castle.

For those interested in vampires, Bran Castle is the place to visit! Vlad the Impaler, the inspiration for Bram Stoker's *Dracula*, was imprisoned there for two months. More recent **architecture** includes the Palace of **Parliament**. Located in Bucharest, it is the second-largest building in the world!

Bran Castle was built in 1377.

Folk art remains a strong part of Romanian **culture**. Brightly colored costumes, woven carpets, and pottery are typical arts. Decorative Easter eggs and painted glass are celebrated Romanian art forms, too.

Romanian folk art features geometric designs, plants, and animals. Different regions often have their own color and design styles for embroidery and woven items.

Folk influences are still heard today in the music of modern composer Gheorghe Enescu. Traditionally, folk music has included dance music, ballads, and pastoral pieces. Key instruments are the violin, the flute, the stringed *cobza*, and the *ţambal*. The *ţambal* is played with small hammers.

Romanians love sports, especially soccer. But, one of Romania's most famous sports stars is gymnast Nadia Comaneci. In 1976, she became the first

Nadia Comaneci won one bronze, one silver, and three gold medals in the 1976 Olympics!

gymnast to receive a score of a perfect ten in the Olympics. That year, she went on to receive seven perfect scores. She was only 14 at the time!

Today, Romanians continue to remember and celebrate their **heritage**. Many still practice traditional arts as proud members of Romanian society.

Painted eggs are one of the most well-known Romanian art forms. This tradition started long ago. Women and children would spend an entire day painting hollow eggs for Easter.

Glossary

alliance - people, groups, or nations joined for a common cause.

Allies - the countries that fought against the Central powers in World War I or the Axis powers in World War II. The World War I Allies were Great Britain, France, and the United States. During World War II, Great Britain, France, the United States, and the Soviet Union were called the Allies.

architecture - the art of planning and designing buildings.

basin - the entire region of land drained by a river and its tributaries.

communism - a social and economic system in which everything is owned by the government and given to the people as needed. A person who believes in communism is called a communist.

constitution - the laws that govern a country.

culture - the customs, arts, and tools of a nation or people at a certain time.

democracy - a governmental system in which the people vote on how to run their country.

economy - the way a nation uses its money, goods, and natural resources.

European Union - an organization of European countries that works toward political, economic, governmental, and social unity.

free enterprise - the freedom of private businesses to operate for profit with little control or regulation by the government.

heritage - the handing down of something from one generation to the next.

humid - having moisture or dampness in the air.

martial law - law administered by the military when civilian enforcement agencies, such as police, can't maintain public order and safety.

NATO - North Atlantic Treaty Organization. A group formed by the United States, Canada, and some European countries in 1949. It tries to create peace among its nations and protect them from common enemies.

Orthodox - a Christian church that developed from the churches of the Byzantine Empire.

Ottoman Empire - an empire created by Turkish tribes that existed from 1300 to 1922. At its height between the 1600s and 1700s, the empire ruled Europe, northern Africa, and the Arabian Peninsula.

parliament - the highest lawmaking body of some governments.

Protestant - a Christian who does not belong to the Catholic Church.

republic - a form of government in which authority rests with voting citizens and is carried out by elected officials, such as those in a parliament.

satellite - a manufactured object that orbits Earth. It relays weather and scientific information back to Earth. It also sends television programs across Earth.

Soviet satellite - a country controlled by the Soviet Union.

vocational - relating to training in a skill or a trade to be pursued as a career.

World War I - from 1914 to 1918, fought in Europe. Great Britain, France, Russia, the United States, and their allies were on one side. Germany, Austria-Hungary, and their allies were on the other side.

World War II - from 1939 to 1945, fought in Europe, Asia, and Africa. Great Britain, France, the United States, the Soviet Union, and their allies were on one side. Germany, Italy, Japan, and their allies were on the other side.

Web Sites

To learn more about Romania, visit ABDO Publishing Company on the World Wide Web at **www.abdopublishing.com**. Web sites about Romania are featured on our Book Links page. These links are routinely monitored and updated to provide the most current information available.

Index